To:
Ryan, Poppy
and Koa
I love you! ♥

DANCE WITH DAISY

Learn how to Promote your Child's Speech & Language Development WHILE READING to them!

Alexandra Princiotta Lowe, MA CCC-SLP

Pediatric Speech Language Pathologist

Illustration by: Febriyana Fadillah

Table of Contents

Introduction

Welcome to The Daisy Speech Books series! Daisy is 2-years-old with a speech delay. Did you know that 2-year-olds typically produce **200-400 words** and are starting to speak in **2-word phrases**!? Daisy's parents and dance teacher use strategies they learned from a speech language pathologist. As you'll see, these strategies can be easily embedded into our daily routines, whether it's a walk outside, morning routines, playtime, and even dance class! One does not need to take a formal dance or movement class. However, it's a wonderful way for children to learn speech and language- specifically body parts, verbs, turn-taking skills, and how to follow instructions. The living room is also a great place to boogie as a family!

The author of this story, a licensed and experienced pediatric speech language pathologist, has had great success using these strategies with children ages 0-3 for over a decade. As a dance teacher herself, she noticed the parallels between speech therapy and dance class, and how movement creates a fun environment to teach children language concepts. Body awareness, imitation skills, self-regulation, and patience are all benefits of dance!

How to Use this Book

This book is to be used as a reference and tool for parents, caregivers, and educators. Come back to The Daisy Speech Books until you can incorporate the strategies without even thinking about it. That's the point! These language tips and tricks should be easily embedded into your daily routines so that as you go about your busy lives, you are simultaneously promoting your child's language development.

Read the strategies or skip ahead to the story. It's up to you! At some point, review the strategies. You will find examples of the language tips throughout the book. You can also use these strategies with typically developing children to support their language development.

New Speech & Language Strategies

1. Let your child lead during play.

We are often so excited to play with our children that we may interrupt what they are already doing. Perhaps they are playing with blocks, but you want to read your child a new book from the library. It takes more 'brain energy' for them to switch activities, and since attention span is quite limited for this age, it would be advantageous to engage with what they are currently doing. If your child is already enjoying an activity, their brains are ready to learn and take in information! Think about how much of their day is planned out for them and chosen by us. Child-led play is a great way to connect, learn language and other concepts, and to tap into their interests. Examples on pages 12, 14.

2. Imitate!

Get your child to imitate you! Whether it's an action or a spoken word, they learn by imitating, and language starts with imitation. You can also imitate your child to elicit turn taking. Turn taking is a vital building block of language. Examples: Imitate your baby making raspberry sounds; get your baby to imitate you waving; imitate your toddler babbling; get your child to imitate you jumping. Examples on pages 15 21, 22, 23, 24.

3. Teach your child signs (American Sign Language).

It is a common misconception that if a child learns to sign, they won't talk. Actually, the opposite is true! The goal (for our language delayed kiddos or babies who are not speaking yet) is not for them to be fluent in American Sign Language, but to use signing as a bridge to spoken language. Signs help babies learn that language is reciprocal- they do or say something and then something else happens in return. This helps decrease frustration for everyone! Always use spoken language with the sign. Recommended signs for babies and toddlers to learn are: "more," "all done," "please," "open," "help." Find the signs Daisy uses in this book on page 35. Examples on pages 13, 14, 18, 28, 30, 31.

4. TEACH, don't TEST!

How many times a day are we asking our babies and toddlers, "what's this?" or "what's that?" It could be frustrating to hear questions all day long, especially if they are not talking yet. Instead, use these opportunities to teach your child the word or concept right away! During bathtime, name your child's body parts out loud. When reading together, point to the objects and actions in the pictures and name them in a fun, singsongy voice. Instead of asking your child the name of their favorite stuffed animal, model what you want your child to say, such as: "Bear is dancing! Bunny is sleeping, shhh!" Examples on pages 21, 25.

5. Create speaking opportunities.

Are your child's favorite toys in reach all day or do they have to ask you for them? Maybe they need to open something in order to get it, or perhaps they can't reach it and they need your help? You can see how in the latter instances, your child needs to use communication somehow to get what they want. They can sign and/or say, "open," "please," or "help." Maybe they are working on speaking at the phrase or sentence level and you can model, "Please open, mama," or, "help me, dada." Note: If your child is not speaking at all yet, teaching signs is a great place to start! Examples on pages 13, 14, 28.

Speech & Language Strategies from *"A Day with Daisy"*

6. Give Choices

Children with language delays often feel frustrated. Offering choices can help your little one feel more in control and therefore regulated (calm and ok!). By giving choices, we are constantly labeling items in their environment, which is important for receptive (understanding) language. Children must understand language before they use language expressively. Example: "Do you want your bunny or your dinosaur for the car ride?" Be sure to hold up both objects in front of your child, that way even if they are not speaking, this can prompt them to point. Examples on pages 16, 27, 33.

7. Sing/Read & Pause

Sing familiar songs with your little one and pause before a word. Continue to sing and pause EVEN if your child does not fill in the words right away. Chances are they will at least pause and look at you- now that you have their attention, say the word. In our electronic world it can be easy to just ask Alexa to play a song, but by singing ourselves we can slow down the rate, pause, sing, and connect as a family! "Twinkle, twinkle little..." The same goes for reading a familiar story. Examples on pages 20, 34.

8. Language Expansion

Add one to three words to what your child says. If your child says, "car," you can respond with, "Cars go beep beep!" Examples on page 19.

9. Talk about what YOU are doing.

The more language exposure the better! One study found that 2-year-olds who were exposed to more talk had larger vocabularies and process language at a faster rate than their peers who heard less words per day (Fernald, 2013). Example: "I'm putting on my shoes because we are going outside!" Example on page 30.

10. Pause & Wait!

While it is true that the more words your child hears the better, it's also important that they are given the opportunity to talk. By pausing and waiting, you are giving your child a chance to respond, thus teaching, "turn taking," which is fundamental for speech and language development. Make a comment or two, and then pause and wait with a smile! Be sure to respond to whatever it is your child did/said to promote turn taking. Try to elicit as many 'back and forth' interactions as you can! Games that teach turn taking are great for demonstrating this; like 'peekaboo' for babies, and rolling a ball back and forth with your toddler. Examples on pages 15, 22, 23, 24, 29.

11. Give Commands to your little one.

Improving their expressive language (talking) is impossible without working on their receptive language (understanding words and their meaning). Typically, 1-year-olds can follow 1-step directions and 2-year olds can follow 2-step directions. In our busy lives, sometimes it's easier to do everything for our little ones, but they learn language and how to be independent by following simple steps. Toddlers feel a sense of satisfaction when they have completed a task, so give them something to do! This can also help with behavior and self-regulation. Ask your toddler to get their shoes instead of getting them yourself. Have them throw something out in the garbage after each meal. Examples on pages 17, 26, 31, 32.

12. Verbal Routines

Verbal Routines are short, repetitive phrases that can be used throughout the day in different contexts. Children anticipate that something is going to happen after the repetitive phrase they are used to hearing (1, 2, 3, or 'ready, set, go') and therefore, will attend to what you are saying. Pause before the last word to give an opportunity to chime in! Examples on page 25.

13. **Parallel Talk.**

Talk about what YOUR CHILD is doing. Be sure to pause so they have an opportunity to speak as well. Make comments instead of asking questions. Examples: "You are feeding the baby." "You are dancing with your dino!" Example on page 26.

14. **Repeat, repeat, repeat!**

Children learn language by hearing a word many times in different contexts. Children who are language delayed often need to hear a word many, MANY times for it to truly "stick." Repetition is key! Instead of talking in long sentences during play, choose a few key words you will target and repeat them as many times as you can! Example: "You are going UP the stairs. Up! Up! Up! We're going... up!" Example on page 32.

15. **Exclamatory words are most certainly words!**

These are words like: "uh oh," "yay," "wee," "yum," and "wow!" To encourage your child to produce exclamatory words, use your facial expressions to exaggerate. Gasping before saying an exclamatory word will help get your child's attention. It's important to have their attention so their brains can take in the information. Exclamatory words are great words to target if your child is not talking that much yet. Example: When you drop something say, "Uh oh!" Example on page 15.

Strategy #1 **Let your child lead during play.**

Notice how dad does not go grab another toy but actively participates in the pretend kitchen environment.

Strategy #3 Teach your child signs.

Here Daisy is signing, 'water.' You can also teach your child the sign for 'drink,' 'milk,' etc.

Strategy #5 Create speaking opportunities.

Note that the water is visible but out of Daisy's reach.

sign: open
1.
2.
Now you want to play with the blocks!
Blocks! Open!
I will open it for you, Daisy.
Strategy #1   Let your child lead during play.
Strategy #5 Create speaking opportunities!
The blocks are kept in a clear container where Daisy needs to ask for help to open them. Keeping toys in clear containers is also a great way to stay tidy. A messy play area can make it difficult for children to attend and benefit from one activity.
Strategy #3 Teach your child signs.
14

I'm going to build a tower.
Nice tower, Daisy. Let's knock it down!
Knock it ...
Down!
YAY!
Strategy #2 Imitate
Strategy #9 Pause & Wait
Strategy #14 Exclamatory Words!

Strategy #6 **Give Choices**

Strategy #10 **Give Commands**

Stretch your vowels and use a sing-songy voice so it is easier for your child to understand and imitate your speech. "Puuut on your shooes."

To teach your child signs, model (do the sign yourself) while saying the word. Be consistent and sign the word at every opportunity. Be patient- it could take many 'teaching opportunities' before your child signs!

Strategy #8 **Language Expansion**

Did you know?

Children that can communicate are 50% less likely to throw a tantrum (Northwestern University, 2019).

Does your child want to sing more of the song? Follow their lead and keep singing!

Ok, class... heels together, happy feet! Let's make a diamond with our legs. Plié!
Bend your knees!
Knees!

Strategy #2 Imitate

Strategy #4 TEACH, don't TEST!

Strategy #2 **Imitate**

Strategy #9 **Pause & Wait**

Strategy #2 Imitate

Strategy #9 Pause & Wait

Strategy #2 **Imitate**

Strategy #9 **Pause & Wait**

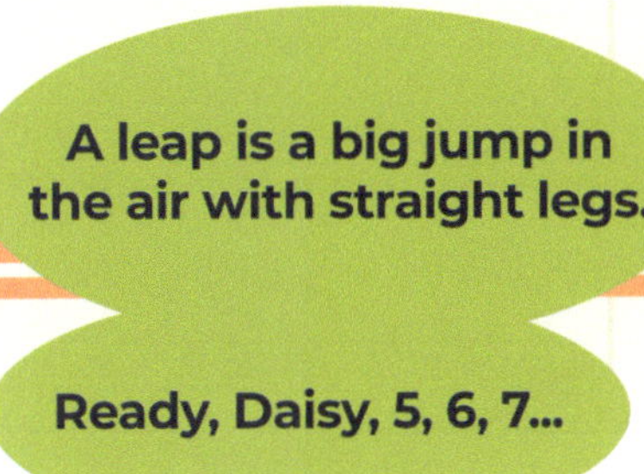

Strategy #4 **TEACH, don't TEST!**

Strategy #11 **Verbal routines**

Verbal routines can be anything... not just '1, 2, 3,' and 'ready, set go!'

Strategy #12 **Parallel Talk**

Strategy #10 **Give Commands**

Playing games like Freeze Dance, Red Light, Green Light, 1, 2, 3, and musical chairs help with impulse control. In order to quickly stop their bodies from moving, children need to be aware of and in control of their bodies. This will help them STOP when running after a ball in the street. Having impulse control also teaches children to regulate their emotions, like not hitting when they are upset.

Strategy #6 **Give Choices**

Strategy #3 **Teach your child signs.**

Strategy #5 **Create speaking opportunities.**

Dad doesn't just hand Daisy her snack right away. He knows she will be hungry; he waits for Daisy to request what she wants on her own. If Daisy didn't request anything, perhaps Dad could munch on some blueberries to prompt her to request.

It's great to talk about what your child did that day. This teaches narration and storytelling skills which are important for language development and are also early literacy skills.

Mama doesn't just fill up Daisy's cup with water, she waits for her to request for more. This has created a speaking opportunity. You'll notice that a lot of the language strategies overlap!

All done, mama!
Ok, Daisy. Here you go. Clean your face and hands, please.
sign: all done
①.
②.

Strategy #3 Teach your child signs.
Strategy #10 Give Commands

Does your child struggle with transitions? Try eliminating the question and just tell them what is happening next. You can let your child know ahead of time, that way it does not come as a big surprise. Routines help children anticipate what's happening next. Most of the time, distraction is the best thing we can do to keep toddlers regulated. Dancing to the next activity is a fun 'distraction!'

Strategy #6 **Give Choices**

Ever notice your little one wants to read the same book over and over? That's great! It's wonderful for their brains to hear the same stories repeatedly because they can anticipate what comes next, which helps develop logical thinking. It is satisfying for children when their predictions are correct.

Another note about reading: Sometimes when little ones are feeling a bit more energetic it is harder for them to sit and listen to an entire story. That's ok! Instead of worrying about reading every word, point to what's on the page and talk about the pictures. Your child will most likely imitate you pointing, which is great since imitation is vital for language! Point to a bird and say, "tweet tweet." Point to the clouds and repeat, "cloud, cloud, cloud" in a fun, slow, sing-songy voice.

Daisy's Signs

sign: water

sign: open

sign: help

sign: please

sign: more

sign: all done

A Note to Parents & Caregivers

Remember that this book is not to replace a speech evaluation or speech therapy, but to act as a useful resource. Reach out to your pediatrician if you are concerned with your child's speech and language development. You can also reach out to your state's early intervention services. In many states, a speech language evaluation and speech therapy are at no cost to the family. If your pediatrician tells you to wait to see if your child 'catches up,' I would seek advice from a licensed speech language pathologist. Current research shows us that the brain is malleable, meaning we can truly shape our children's brains by creating new neural pathways, especially from birth to 3-years-old, therefore the earlier the intervention, the better!

The strategies you have learned from this book are meant to be embedded into your daily routines. They should not feel forced. If you are feeling overwhelmed by the strategies, just pick 1 or 2 to do in certain environments, like bath time or on a walk. Connect with your child and enjoy your time together, engaging in back-and- forth interactions throughout the day. The fact that you have this book shows you are already doing your best to promote your child's language development!

Notes & Resources

Anne Fernald's elegant study: Anne Fernald, Virginia A. Marchman, and Adriana Weisleder, "SES differences in language processing skill and vocabulary are evident at 18 months," _Developmental Science_ 16.2 (2013): 234-248.

Mize, L. (2011). _Teach me to talk: The therapy manual; a comprehensive guide for treating receptive and expressive language delays and disorders in toddlers and young preschoolers_. Teachmetotalk.com.

Speech & Language Milestones

https://www.cdc.gov/ncbddd/actearly/milestones/milestones-in-action.html

https://ncdc.ca/services-for-children/speech-and-language-therapy/

Northwestern University. (2019, November 11). Late talkers twice as likely to have severe, frequent temper tantrums. ScienceDaily. Retrieved March 29, 2024 from www.sciencedaily.com/releases/2019/11/191111133322.html

About the Author

Alexandra Princiotta Lowe is a licensed speech language pathologist with her own private practice. She has a passion for helping families feel confident in providing language rich environments for their children. Alex works with children of all ages in both California and New York- thanks to telehealth! She also works with people with aphasia.

Alex lives in Los Angeles, California, with her husband, and two children, Penelope (Poppy) and Koa. You might find Alex on the beach with her family. Follow her on Instagram - @akp_speechtherapy!

www.akpspeech.com